WORDS OF ENCOURAGEMENT

Notes of Instructions
delivered by
Daniel Considine, SJ
arranged by Rev. F. Devas

CATHOLIC TRUTH SOCIETY
PUBLISHERS TO THE HOLY SEE

CONTENTS

FOREWORD

These *Words of Encouragement* are selections made from various notes taken of Father Considine's instructions and conferences, and from letters written by him; and the section bearing here the title *The Great Mystery* is from a report, revised by him, of a sermon he preached at the Farm Street church in London, on the Feast of Corpus Christi, 1921.

Father Considine's manner was marked by extraordinary simplicity and directness: if he had a platitude to repeat, he did not attempt to disguise it in fine language; on the other hand, in the interest of the particular audience he was addressing, he did not hesitate to stress a particular point of view or a particular truth with sometimes an apparent disregard for other points of view and other truths, which to the casual reader may prove disconcerting. Thus it would be difficult to discover in a textbook of dogmatic theology the scholastic equivalent of his statement in *Sorrow* that 'God is shy': while the lukewarm and frivolous might easily take to themselves false comfort when reading in Distractions in Prayer that 'to resign myself to a distraction for God's sake is union with God'.

4

But Father Considine was not addressing theologians as theologians, but as seekers after perfection; nor was he addressing the lukewarm and the frivolous, but those whom he believed to be over-anxious in their approach to our Blessed Lord.

The practical and immediate needs of the individual, and an individual always earnest and honest, but often timid and puzzled, were the object of Father Considine's solicitude; such individuals will find now in his written words what others found in them when they were first spoken – not only encouragement but also enlightenment.

F.C.D.

WORDS OF ENCOURAGEMENT

'Last came forward the man who had the one talent. "Sir," he said, "you entrusted me with two talents; here are two more that I have made." *Mt* 25, 24.

Unworthy thoughts about God

If we don't look upon God as a hard man we have every reason to congratulate ourselves. We say we think Him merciful, kind, loving, but in our hearts we look upon Him as hard. Three-quarters of the troubles of good people come from this. He feels intensely our misconception of Him. We look upon Him as a hard, grasping man, who wants to get all He can out of us and give nothing in return. And woe betide us if we fail to satisfy Him. This is utterly wrong.

If God has ever shown me any love He must love me still. God does not care for me one day and hate me the next. He is not capricious or inconstant like man. Above everything, God wants my love, and with love comes happiness and enthusiasm in His service. We think: I have only one talent, others have five. Therefore I will do nothing but bury mine. I will run no risks. But each of our temperaments and characters has been fitted exactly, thought out from all time to suit our lives. What others have would not suit me. What we have we don't value; what we have not we desire. Do not say, God evidently, from my capabilities, does not care much for me; does not expect much from me. God craves your love. Ask, ask, ask for graces and you will assuredly get them.

A Wrong Kind of Sorrow

Do not cry over spilt milk. Do not dwell on the faults and mistakes of the past. Leave them alone; leave them to God. As soon as possible make an Act of Contrition and never think of them again. Often the despondence caused by sin is more wrong, and keeps one away from God more than the sin itself. Don't waste time being discouraged. Get up and go to God. Draw near to Him. Do not stand back hanging your head.

Do what you are doing. Some people always have one eye on the past and the other on the future, instead of both on the present. Don't waste time deploring the past and being apprehensive of the future. Grace will be given to meet each day the difficulties of that day. There are very few people who would not be good at their own job if they would only develop the power of concentration. It is this incessant worrying over past and future that prevents the concentration. Leave the future in God's hands.

Think of God in goodness. Have a good opinion of God. God loves us to think well of Him, to trust Him, to think lovingly of Him. Do not think God does not forgive easily. The more intimate a human friendship the less nervous one is of a chance word offending one's friend. Friends are not lost for ever by some little word or act displeasing them. Above all, remember that in darkness, gloom, dejection, or depression God does not dwell. Do not even make acts of sorrow, if that depresses; make acts of hope and love. Depression never comes from God; neither does any thought which makes His service difficult. Have always the highest opinion of Our Lord and Master.

The Yoke of the Lord

Perhaps of all the qualities the one most desired by Our Lord and prized above every other is submission. Nothing so impedes our progress as putting our will in opposition to His. Holiness consists in trying to fit ourselves to listen to the very first promptings of the Holy Spirit, and then in trying to carry out God's Will. Complete submission is of the very first importance. It means being ready to do whatever God asks, whenever and however He asks us. We often complain that He does not show us His Will. But this is because God will not show us His Will if He knows we will not comply with His wishes. He will not tell us what He wants if He sees we are not ready to do it. The Incarnation teaches us submission. Our Lord was treated as a baby, a boy, and a man, always subject to His parents. Yet all the time He was God. If we are restless or rebellious we should think of this. Our Lord cannot let us go about His Father's business in our own way. We must be submissive and go His way. We cannot make terms and conditions with Him; our terms are too imperfect, therefore He cannot grant them. We should say: 'Lord, I give You my heart as a tablet on which nothing is written. Write Your will on it.' Do not have pet schemes for the improvement of yourself or the race. Have no will of your own; give your will into God's hands and leave it there. Examine yourself as to whether you are absolutely and entirely submissive to God's will. You should be willing to serve God for the love of serving Him, not for wages. Than which I can wish you no greater blessing.

'So for tomorrow and its needs
I do not pray;
But keep me, guide me, love me,
Just for today.'

Spiritual Energy

Job says the life of man upon earth is a continual warfare, or conflict. So no matter how far we are advanced in the spiritual life, we must never expect immunity from temptation; from ups and downs. St Paul in his 1st Epistle to the Corinthians says: 'Everyone runs, but not everyone gets a prize. Everyone that strives for the mastery must

refrain himself from many things'. St Paul is addressing a
people who lived on the Isthmus of Corinth, a place
famous at that time for beauty, art, luxury and,
consequent on the latter, profligacy. But also a spot
rendered famous by the games which took place there.
For this reason St Paul likens the spiritual life to games,
to a race. He is not addressing those who sit under an
awning watching and gently applauding the efforts of the
athletes. He speaks to those who take part in the race. It is
an image of the spiritual life, which entails effort,
exertion, and often exhaustion. Our Lord says: Work out
your salvation; traffic until I come. He wants effort,
untiring effort. The Curé d'Ars used to say when people
spoke of his holiness, 'I'm not afraid of trouble, that is
all'. Not meaning trouble in the sense of sorrow, but in
the sense of labour, fatigue. We are dreadfully afraid of
trouble; otherwise we should be much nearer to Our Lord
than we are. Man is by nature an extremely lazy animal,
who likes nothing so much as to do nothing. I do not
mean in a physical sense. Sometimes in a sermon or a
book we hear or see something we think exactly fits
ourselves. We make a resolution to carry it out, which we
do until it costs us something. We resolve to cultivate
recollection, which we do until we hear some really spicy
bit of scandal, then the recollection is thrown to the
winds. I should ask myself from month to month what
good are these instructions doing me? If I feel tired and

battered, that is no reason for dissatisfaction. A soldier in a campaign is not astonished if he is wounded or feels overdone from fatigue. Neither must I say in my sphere of life there is no work open to me. There is always work. If I have a bad temper there is plenty of work cut out for me for years to come. If we have that dangerous gift of saying smart things, when even our best friends have the benefit of our wit at their expense, that is a thing to fight against. I should fight like a true soldier – full of courage, full of high hopes. Finally, do not be astonished if there are storms, if there is opposition, if friends say, 'Why, what has come to So-and-so? She is becoming a perfect nuisance with her piety. Why this fervour all of a sudden?' For in a seemingly monotonous, uneventful, unsuccessful life, there may be more peace, joy, and true happiness than in that of a person who is surrounded with every luxury, every satisfaction, and the love and admiration of everyone with whom she comes in contact.

Practical Self-Denial

St Paul says: 'I will chastise my body and bring it into subjection, lest, having preached to others, I myself become a castaway'. It is great mistake to think that without bodily austerities we cannot draw very near to God. Without bodily austerities we can withdraw all obstacles between Himself and ourselves; we can get a very intimate knowledge of Him and can please Him very much. He will not keep His choicest gifts from us because of the way in which we are circumstanced. In the days of great austerity nerves did not exist. They are a product of our time. Nerves are the austerities we have to bear today. Bear with yourself, your depression, gloom, moods, variability of temper. To bear with one's self is an act of great virtue. A very great deal of evil comes from the fact that a fit of nerves is so often mistaken for something wrong with the soul. To use an expression so common amongst youngsters nowadays, we feel rotten. Not to lose patience with ourselves when we feel rotten is a very high virtue. The worst form of nerves is depression. People really believe that they have lost faith, hope, love, everything. It is a very great trial. St Teresa says: 'The worst of sickness is that it so weakens you, you cannot fix your thoughts on God'. But this is of no consequence. It is the doing for God that is important, not the thinking of God. It is a very great trial to many of us to be unable to get every day to Holy Communion. But to bear quietly with our weakness, because it is His will, pleases Him a great deal more than the most fervent Communion we ever made. Headaches are a great trial. We cannot pray with a 'head'; but if we bear with ourselves it is more meritorious than the best of prayers. Bear with others. We most of us have a great deal to bear from others. It is often the reflex of what they have to bear from us, but still, none the less, very hard. The people we live with are not omniscient. They may be excellent, and have the best intentions, but they make mistakes; they may form hard judgments. Let us ask God to give us patience to bear with ourselves and to bear with others.

The Lord is with You

We ought to go through the world holding God's hand. There is much suffering that has to be gone through in this life, and it makes all the difference of pleasure or pain whether we have our hand in God's or not. It will make a joy of even mortification. The Angel Gabriel said to Our Lady, The Lord is with you. We ought to make the intention, every time we say the Hail Mary, of asking Our Lord to be with us. Try and love God. He wants us all to be saints. It is our own fault if we are not. In spite of darkness and despondency we must keep on asking Him to be with us. The troubles I have are the troubles He had. For instance, monotony. He was year after year a common carpenter; not even a joiner. Everything He did He did in the hope that we should imitate Him. Bear the burden of life cheerfully, and we are more than half-way to being saints. If God treats us in the way that He treated Mary and her Son we should be only too pleased. Health, money, success are not His best gifts. He rarely gives them to His dearest friends. We say, I should like to be settled in life; have more money, beauty, talents. Are you certain they would be good for you? If so, He would certainly give them to you. Our Lord is always wondering how He can best help us to love Him. If you find life difficult, tell Him so; hard to be good, tell Him so. You are suffering, or at any rate you cannot pray – you regret it – tell God so, that is prayer. If you try to do these things of your own strength you will never succeed. If you go through life holding His hand, love will make everything easy.

Trust in the Lord

'Directly after this he made the disciples get into the boat and go on ahead to the other side while he would send the crowds away.' (*Mt* 14:22). A voyage thus begun we should have thought would be most prosperous, undertaken by a direct command of Our Lord Himself. The Disciples embarked and began their journey in order to do the Will of God. Surely it will be a most favourable one!

On the contrary, they met an adverse wind, rough seas, and everything that was difficult. 'While the boat, by now far out on the lake, was battling with a heavy sea, for there was a head-wind.' (*Mt* 14:24). The sea raged, the wind howled, the little boat was tossed about – and Jesus was not there! Our Lord was with them, but it was His Will they should have this difficulty. It is necessary to meet many troubles in His service: even when we are most truly doing His Will.

Our Lord allowed these tribulations to befall His
Disciples in order to show His watchful love over them.
He allows troubles to befall us in order to make us long
for Him, think of Him, turn to Him, trust in Him, and call
upon Him for help.

Far from losing courage, we ought to redouble our
efforts in His service and work fearlessly, however loudly
the winds and the waves may roar. He sees and knows all,
and awaits His own time. In His own time He will come,
even walking on the waters of tribulation.

'In the fourth watch of the night He went towards
them, walking on the lake, and when the disciples saw
Him walking on the lake they were terrified. "It is a
ghost" they said, and cried out in fear. But at once Jesus
called out to them, saying, "Courage! It is I! Do not be
afraid."'(*Mt* 14:25-27). Often in trouble we cry out, and
He answers in our hearts. He often comes to us in that
very tribulation which hides Him from us saying:
'Courage!: it is I! Do not be afraid'.

Peter, full of impetuous love, hearing the voice of his
Master, cries out, 'Lord, if it is You, tell me to come to
You across the water'. (*Mt* 14:28). Tell me to come to
You! And He said 'Come'! Then Peter walked upon the
water to come to Jesus. Fervent love offers itself for any
service, believes nothing impossible, is ready for all.

St Peter walks happily towards Jesus as long as he
looks at Him alone, but the moment he looks at the waves

and himself he sinks. Look at Jesus, not at self or at danger. Then St Peter cried out: 'Lord, save me!' And immediately Jesus stretched out His hand, took hold of him, and said 'Man of little faith, why did you doubt?' Jesus and Peter entered the boat. And the wind ceased; calm reigned around. Then they adored Jesus, saying: 'Truly, You are the Son of God'.

Divine Providence

'My days are in Your hand.' (*Ps* 30:15). Suppose, my God, You had told us that, as we know the worth of our soul, You were going to trust us with the choice of the means by which its salvation is to be worked out; You were going to put before us riches and poverty, sickness and health, success and failure, a long life and a short one, and we might take that which seemed best for us. Should we be content? Should we not say, if we were wise: 'My God, do not trust this to me. I shall choose, I know I shall, what I like, not what is best for me.'

And suppose You were to tell us there were souls to whom You would not entrust such a decision. Either they were too weak, or You were so anxious to save them that You had left the choice of means not to themselves but to those who love them better than they love themselves, and who would choose for them more wisely. To their Guardian Angel, to their Patron Saint, even to the Seat of Wisdom herself; and if we wished You would let us be one of those favoured souls. Should we be content, then? Or should we say: 'My God, forgive me for being mistrustful still. I know my Guardian Angel and my holy Patrons and, most of all, my Mother Mary, love me dearly and would do their best for me; but their wisdom after all is not infinite. They might make a mistake, and that mistake might mean the loss of everything to me. I cannot afford any risk here. My soul is my only one; I must save it whatever happens. I dare not keep it in my hands, and I dare not trust it even to the highest and holiest and wisest of those around Your throne.'

And suppose again You were to say to us: 'There are a few, a very few, whose salvation is so dear to Me that I will trust the choice of means to no one. I will plan and arrange all Myself. Nothing shall happen to them but what has been foreseen and prepared from all eternity by My infinite Wisdom and Goodness. No one shall touch them, no joy or sorrow shall come in their way, no, nor a hair of their head fall to the ground without My knowledge and permission.' Should we not cry out: 'My God, I hardly dare ask it, but oh that I might be one of that happy chosen few, for surely they are safe!'

You check me by a warning: 'These souls will not have all their own way in life. Their road will sometimes be hard and rugged. They will see things prosper in the hands of others and fail in theirs. They will be hardly used by those around them – misjudged, set aside, unjustly treated; life to many of them will be uphill work.' Do I draw back now, or do I cry out again: 'No matter that, no matter that at all! What will they care when they know Your arm is around them as they go uphill; Your hand sends the cross, and the failure, and the pain! No, my God, that does not frighten me. Let me be only one of those whose lot is altogether in Your hands, and I will fear nothing; no, I will be grateful for all that comes to me. I will kiss Your hand even when You strike me. I shall feel peaceful and happy always in the thought that it is the wisdom of my God that orders all for me, and the love of my Heavenly Father that provides everything to help me. Let me be one of those chosen ones, and You will see how I value my privilege, how I prize whatever You send.'

Suppose – I have been saying. But this is no supposition. I am that privileged one whose life in its minutest details is Your ordering and Your care. How can I complain, my God? How can I be mistrustful or even anxious? 'My days are in Your hand.'

Devotion to the Sacred Heart

The great object of the devotion to the Sacred Heart is that it should teach us to love Our Lord because He loves us. We were brought into the world solely because He loved us, and He wanted our love. He wants to do us good. He longs to do us good. He wants to know us, and wants us to

know Him. He longs to heap His love upon us, to draw us
very near to Him. We tie His hands by our coldness, our
callousness, our indifference. We have such a wrong idea
of Him. He is not always on the look out to catch us
tripping; or wanting to keep us persistently in suspense as
to whether we shall save our souls. 'Do I love God?' you
are probably thinking. 'Of course I love God, but in a
common-sense, practical way. I must not be carried away
by hysterical excesses. Religion must fill a certain part of
my life but no more. If I let myself go there is no knowing
where it might end. I shall finish by finding myself in a
convent or some other equally unpleasant place.' This is
the view of the common-sense Catholic. Am I a common-
sense Catholic or an enthusiastic Catholic?

From our childhood many of us have been told so
much more of the punishments God has in store for us if
we fail to please Him than of the rewards He looks
forward to giving when we do please Him. In preparing
for Confession we spend nine minutes in examining our
conscience and one minute in telling Our Lord we are
sorry. The first thing necessary in loving Our Lord is to
believe Him lovable. What are the sort of persons one
loves? First, they must be easy to get on with. How many
in their heart of hearts think Our Lord easy to get on with?
We think Him touchy, unapproachable, easily annoyed or
offended. And yet all this fear of Him pains Him very
much. Would our father wish us to hang our heads, be shy

and shrinking in his presence? How much less so our Heavenly Father? He has an almost foolish love for us. Never was a mother so blind to the faults of her child as Our Lord is to ours. He makes allowances to an almost extravagant degree. He is infinitely quicker to pity and help than to blame and punish. Whatever attracts you in your fellow-creatures is His gift, and possessed by Him in a higher sense. And yet how many ascribe to Him mean and petty ways, trying to catch us out, to be ungenerous, conduct we would not tolerate in human friendship. There is nothing easier than to love God, because there is nothing unlovable in Him. God is Love. He asks our love in return. Oh, my God, fill my heart, my soul, my whole being with the fire of Your Divine Love. You, oh my God, are the God of my heart, and my portion for ever.

The Habit of Perfection

There seems to be a general persuasion that God is difficult to please; that He is hard, severe, unfair. Some have too much money; others in a state of abject poverty. This is unfair, so I shall not try to please Him. The poor cannot have oyster suppers, neither can they have *paté de foie gras* for lunch. But this is not the fault of our Heavenly Father. Squalor, poverty, and degradation are the result of sin. The real pleasures of life are open to all: love, social life in the different spheres of society, enjoyment of nature, mountains, trees, flowers, good health.

We all have a millstone hanging about our necks. We say: 'The perfect service of God is not meant for me; for others, yes, but not for me. My past or my present prevents me from ever doing anything for God. I have felt that I was meant for something good, but I did not take the opportunity. Now it is useless; I shall never do anything.' Is it true that we can do nothing for God because we have not done so from the cradle? At the present moment you have a desire to please and love God. From whom does that desire come? We can't have a desire to love God unless He gives us that desire. Would God encourage us along a path which ended with 'No Thoroughfare'? We do not see that cool wind which fans our cheeks, and yet we feel the movement in the atmosphere. Thus it is with grace. In one moment He can transform the most abandoned heart into one full of love for Him. Some say: 'I don't feel that God wants me to love Him; He doesn't care whether I love Him or not'. Our Lord died for each one of us. Could He do more? He longs for our personal love. High sanctity is within the reach of everyone. Our Lord does not look to beauty, position, money, intellect. All He asks is correspondence to His grace. That, and that alone, is all that is necessary to become a saint. Others say: 'I've tried to love Our Lord. I still find no remedy against distractions'; or, 'I love the pleasures of life, the comforts money can buy'; or, 'I am still bored with so-and-so'. Our Lord Himself disliked heat and cold. He resented being struck in the face, and said: 'Why do you strike Me?' Others say: 'I cannot be recollected'. What is this recollection? Do people living in a busy city expect to pass their life in a kind of trance? Walking down Piccadilly you do not say with every step 'I am walking down Piccadilly', and yet you are doing so. You cannot be perpetually saying, 'I am being recollected'. All you have to do is to ask Our Lord to live in the centre of your heart, to stay with you. He will undoubtedly and assuredly respond to your invitation. Let us ask Him to make our hearts His home always and for ever.

The Spirit of Joy

We should all do very much more for God if we endeavoured to bring more enjoyment into our lives and into the lives of others. If the world were much better it would be much happier. St Paul says, 'Rejoice in the Lord always, and again I say rejoice'. Happiness always leads to and never away from God. If we are inclined to be superior and look down on mirth and joy, there is something very wrong with our view of the spiritual life. We also do infinite harm to religion. The world looks upon piety as in some way connected with sadness. As laughter is good for the body, so is cheerfulness good for the soul. People will say, 'We are not told that Our Lord ever laughed'. On the other hand, we are told that Our

Lord was loved wherever he went. And who is so little loved as a wet-blanket, who carries a damping atmosphere of gloom and depression wherever he goes? It is no sign of sanctity to fail to find pleasure and amusement in what pleases and amuses others. Let us make our own service of God as easy as possible. He Himself has said, 'My yoke is sweet and My burden light. Come to Me and I will refresh you.'

Patience and Perseverance

One of the greatest mistakes we make in the spiritual life is in lack of preparation. We are all in such a hurry to be better, to be holy. Half the secret of success in teaching consists in repetition, yet no one wants to repeat. No one likes the grind of the grammar. In our spiritual life we want to skip declensions, genders, verbs and syntax. We want to get into close relationship with God. We expect to pray with no distractions. We want to read God's secrets before we can spell. God's friends are, above all, humble; we want grounding, we want spade-work. We don't prepare ourselves for the inspirations of the Holy Spirit. We wonder, after the way we have tried, that we are not better. Very different from the saints, who are always thanking God that they are not worse. If you really are going forward you probably think you are going backward. If you open the door of a dark room you cannot see the dust or dirt that is in it. But if you open even a chink of the shutter, then it is that you see the dust. The more light you let in the more dust you notice. Thus it is with God's light. The more we ask the Holy Spirit to pour His illuminating light into our souls, the more we notice our faults.

'Thrice Blessed Light, shoot home Your darts,

And pierce the centres of those hearts

Whose faith aspires to You.'

In the good old days you had no faults. Everyone else had lots. 'So-and-so is so selfish', 'so bumptious', 'so uncharitable'. The better you become the more good you see in others. God did not think four thousand years too long a time in which to prepare the world for the coming of His Son. St John the Baptist says, 'The axe is put to the root'. Let us put the axe to the root of those faults which keep us from Our Lord. It is not the reading of pious books, or the saying of long prayers, or science, or knowledge, which introduces the Child Jesus into our hearts. It is the love, it is the longing for Him to be there, that brings Him. It is the real effort that it costs us to put the axe to the root. We know what He loves, we know what He dislikes. If you want Him you must not be afraid to pay the price. Let us ask Our Lord what faults we are to try to get rid of by way of preparation to receiving Him into our hearts.

Diffidence and Generosity

Am I using to the full the grace God gives me? Have I any reason for supposing that God wants me to lead a better life than hitherto? Does He want to come into my heart? Is it not a little presumptuous, rather emotional, to think that Our Lord really wants to make my Heart his own? In order to make no one nervous, I will say at once that in speaking of God's calls I do not mean in any sense a call to religious life. The feeling of unrest, of spiritual dissatisfaction; the feeling that I've not really got hold of the one thing which can fill my life; the sensation of the emptiness, hollowness of the world: these feelings do not come from myself, still less do they come from the Devil. Why should we wish to stir up still waters? They are calls from God. If these thoughts take shape in my mind it is a certain indication that God wants more of me. He wants me to draw nearer to Him, to do better. Our Lord has different ways of calling different people. St Andrew and St John were walking with St John the Baptist, who said, 'Behold the Lamb of God'. John and Andrew followed after Our Lord and asked Him where He was lodging. Our Lord said, 'Come and see'. They went with Him, stayed all night, and next morning said: 'Now we have found the Messiah'. St Peter was called while mending his nets. The rich young man said, 'Good Master, what must I do to possess eternal life?' 'Keep the commandments.' 'I do so.' Our Lord looked at him and loved him. 'Then if you would be perfect, go sell all you have and give to the poor, and come follow Me.' The Evangelist tells us he went away sad, because he had a great deal of property. Our Lord calls us each in our different way. I am not speaking of a religious vocation, but a call to lead a better life. Our Lord says. 'I want you to become a special friend of Mine; to break with whatever you know to be unworthy of you. I want you to be perfect, to be willing to sell all you have to follow Me'. I am not speaking of selling all in a literal sense. Our Lord says, 'If you want to be perfect you must let nothing stand between you and Me; there must be nothing held back: no deliberate affection for anything opposed to My Will'. The standard is high, but Our Lord's words are, 'If you would be perfect'. Are there things in my heart which pull me away from Our Lord? What has been stopping me from real peace of soul? Am I too fond of admiration? Do I set too much store on the affection of others? Some of us hear the voice of God loud enough to make us uncomfortable and still we won't give in. Is there anything I am holding back? Am I quite happy? quite satisfied? He asks: 'Are you willing to give Me anything I want? To do whatever I ask of you? Come follow Me'. He who made our hearts knows how to attract them. Misery is the element of Satan. Joy is the element of Our Lord. The highest joy is to be found in His service. He wants us to be near Him, because to be near Him is happiness. He wants us to be like Him, because to be like Him is happiness. He wants us to become less selfish; to think more of others, more of Him; to love Him and to help others to love Him. Is He not worth following? Beg of Him to make His call so clear as to be unmistakable, and have the generosity to be content, and even anxious, to follow wherever He may lead.

Reflections on the Old Year

It would be well for us all at the beginning of a new year to look back quietly upon the year that has just disappeared. The one thing that is of importance for me to discover is: What opinion has God of me? What am I to learn from last year? Am I satisfied with the recollection of it? There are three ways in which we might review it. One class of person might say: 'Well, I have every reason to be pleased with myself. I have done uncommonly well.' I am afraid this usually would mean that that person's standard was deplorably low; that his view was shallow and flippant. Another person might say: 'So last year is over. It was very much like the previous year, and next year will be very much the same. It has been a dull year, but not so dull as next year will probably prove itself to be.' Of all the hopeless people to deal with, the person who finds life dull is the most hopeless. He is a person who has never put his shoulder to the wheel. God says in the Apocalypse, 'I wish you were either hot or cold'. If you are cold there may be some chance that the fact of your being so may be brought home to you, and you may try to get warm. But if you are lukewarm you do not feel the cold, and you do not ask for heat. You lounge through life yawning and moaning, saying: 'I suppose I shall have the same old treadmill round of duties, same old boring jobs to be got through'. Our Lord says: 'What have you done for Me the year just past? What victories have you made? Do you love Me? Have you tried to overcome yourself? To help others? Are you a better person? Have you more will-power than you had? How much time have you dreamed away in useless imaginings?' And still a third class of person might say: 'I am more sorry than I can say, but even in my self-abasement I am grateful to you for letting me see it.' This is the spirit of God within us. Perhaps you will say. 'There are others more jealous, selfish, careless, lazy than I am'. Then you are comparing yourself with the wrong persons. It is possible there are others more full of faults than you are, though I hope not so conceited. But compare yourself with Our Lord and then see how you stand. What were your fears and hopes at the beginning of last year? For such and such a month you were obsessed by such and such a fear. How many of your anticipated troubles ever came into existence? How much time have we given to brooding over troubles which never took shape? When asked to advise a friend, how often have we found out what she wanted us to say and then said it, in order to be considered a charming, sympathetic person, quite regardless of what was for her good? Why do we continually and for ever wear a mask? even with God Himself. Which of us can say that he has not been enormously swayed by the thought of 'What will my own little world say?' 'What will So-and-so think of my decision?' If we could only put this cowardice aside and endeavour always to do what we think right, even at the cost of pain to those we love very dearly. Is it not better to please the Creator than the creature? God does not open our eyes to unpleasant truths unless He wants us to profit by them. Do let us become, in the best sense of the word, independent. Let us go to God rather than to the world for advice and for courage.

Looking Forward

We all make mistakes. What we ought to do is to try to profit by them. How am I to find out what God wants me to do? St Paul said: 'Lord, what would You have me do?' If we say this from our hearts Our Lord never refuses an answer. Some people never do ask it. Others don't ask with perfect sincerity. They are not determined to do whatever He should ask them. We need never be afraid. If we really want to please God we shall do so. St Thomas Aquinas, on being asked the shortest way to love God, said: 'To want to love Him'. If we want to overcome pride, obstinacy, sloth, we shall do so. If in the past I have been conceited and selfish. If I want to overcome these faults in the future, I can do so. We cannot all be in *Debrett*. We cannot all be intimate with the aristocracy. We seem, many of us, to consider that those laws which hold good in social life apply also to the spiritual life. That it is only a certain select few who are really called upon to love God, to become intimate with Our Lord. That for the ordinary mortal such an idea is pure presumption. We look up to loving God as we would look up to Mont Blanc. The eternal snows bathed in sunshine, radiant, stupendous, magnificent, but inaccessible and unapproachable. And God is every hour trying to draw you nearer to Him, and you are trying to draw back. 'Lord, what would You have me do?' First, to be satisfied with your lot in life. Not to want to be richer, cleverer, prettier. Who is responsible for every detail of your life? God. If you are discontented, it is, in plain English, rebellion against God's Will. Find me the person who is absolutely satisfied and you will find a saint. Let us make it a rule always to try and be satisfied. What an effect it would have on our lives. Wet or fine, ill or well, rich or poor. Don't blame God. And about my spiritual state? I ought to be eager to get on; but even that I should leave in His hands. Be satisfied even with your spiritual state. If God does not want you to go forward more quickly than you are doing, do not wish to do so. He does not wish us to become saints in a day. He wishes a virtue to grow. Acting up to grace means doing the easy things that come our way, doing them well, and doing them humbly because they are His Will. Thus do we become saints.

In his fifth chapter St John tells us how Our Lord cured the man who had lain for no less than thirty-eight years by the pool, waiting to be the first into the water after the Angel had stirred it. When we think of the years we have lived and the little we have accomplished, may we not justly compare ourselves with that poor man? Year after year he fails to reach the water first and, heaving a sigh, hopes for better luck next time. Year after year we have been slack in the service of God. Year after year we refuse to listen to His constant appeals to us to be better. Are we not waiting for the moving of the water? When God sends His Angel to touch the pool of our soul, in which He should be, but is not always, mirrored, should we not listen to Him? Do we not often say: 'It is hardly of any use my trying to reach the pool of God's grace. I may as well lie here. Others always get there first. I am too slow and dull to try. I have little belief in His love for and interest in me.' We ought to say: 'After all, it is not so difficult to love God. If He laid down His life for me, He must love me a little bit. If not a single thought passes through my mind that has not passed through God's mind, does it not show He cares for me?' Remorse is the lover's expostulation for not having trusted more. There is only one person who can teach us to love God, that is God

Himself. If you do not think Him lovable, you cannot love Him. Religion is the service of God, is love of God. He is everything that is likable, lovable, and easy to get on with. If you think Him haughty, far away and unapproachable, you invest Him with unlovable qualities and you will not love Him. The Devil says: 'You are unfitted for His service, a coward. He offered you a mortification; you did not take it. You are weary in well-doing. You are not one of the elite called to Divine love.' He wishes us to think of our Master as hard, difficult to please; that we must for ever be on our best behaviour. How different to the Apostles, who were so completely at home with Him. What is the talisman for the future? It is to have a true opinion of Our Lord. Not to think Him difficult, pompous, hard, but generous, willing, ever eager to forgive, and always finding more to pity than to blame in us. Ask Our Lord to help us to know Him, for to know Him is to love Him.

Familiarity with Our Lord

We have great difficulty in not looking at Our Lord as a high and mighty Personage. We should try hard to realise that Our Lord in His Humanity felt just as we feel. Tired, weary, hungry. When left alone inclined to take a dismal view of life. Tempted to despondency. Our Lord likes us to show Him sympathy. He in His life on earth was just as appreciative of every particle of sympathy offered Him as we should be. Never the smallest kindness done to Him was unnoticed. He hungered for love and sympathy. In the house of Simon how He appreciated Mary Magdalene's ministrations. He said to Simon, who was pretending not to notice Mary Magdalene, 'When I entered your house you gave Me no water for My feet. This woman with her tears has washed them, and with her hair has wiped them. You gave Me no kiss; this woman has never ceased to kiss My feet.' We do not realise how much Our Lord has had to bear for us. The one thing He desired when He came into the world was to do good to souls. If we have one great object in life, and that object is thwarted, what a crushing sorrow it is. And yet Our Lord was thwarted at every turn. His preaching was misunderstood; His miracles and cures He got no thanks for. The one thing He looked for, to gain love, failed Him. Take Our Lord's day; it was one long string of disappointments. And how we grumble over our trifling, futile, little disappointments. How ungenerous, how mean we are.

When you think of your disappointments, compare them with Our Lord's. The way to be happy is to look at things from His point of view. His efforts invariably met with failure. When He had explained fully about His Body and Blood (John 6), we are told that 'many of them ceased to walk with Him'. What a sorrow for Him. Then it was that, feeling crushed and worn out, He said St Peter: 'Will you also leave Me?' And Peter answered: 'To whom, Lord, shall we go, for You have the words of eternal life?' What a disappointment even the Apostles were. At the end even of the third year of His ministry how imperfect they were, how little credit they did Him. They had arrived at no greater understanding of Him than to think still that He was to be the Founder of an earthly kingdom, and at no greater virtue than to be wrangling as to who were to have the best places. If Our Lord were to say to anyone here: 'I will, if you choose it, give you a life of perfect happiness; everyone shall try to please you, everything you touch succeed', I trust there is no one here who would not say: 'No, Lord; what was good enough for You is good enough for me'. These thoughts should throw a flood of light on our lives. If we wish to imitate Our Lord and Master, instead of crying our eyes out in moments of gloom and despondency, we should say: 'What You do is for the best, I will not wish it otherwise. When I am cowardly and inclined to cry out under suffering; if I ask for the pain to be removed – do not take me at my word, Lord, but give me greater strength and so draw me nearer to You'.

'Why are you fearful, O you of little faith?'

'Every word of God is fire-tried, and He is a Buckler of Hope to those who hope in Him.' (Proverbs). This means that every word of God is absolutely true, and that He is a shield or protector to those who hope in Him. What is the hope most people have in Him? Withered, shrunk, ineffective. (I am not, of course, speaking of the theological virtue on which our salvation depends, but of hope in God's help in the everyday episodes of our life.) Religion should be a part of one's life. It consists in always thinking of God. The whole day long. Our Lord wants to be Master of your heart, and Master all the day long. Our Lord lives in your heart. He does not want you to tell Him in so many words that you love Him; He knows you cannot be praying all day. But He wants you always to be thinking of Him, to feel that He is with you. People are not intimate with Him because they think they can't be, so they don't try. Our Lord says: 'My yoke is sweet and My burden is light'. And again: 'Come to Me all you who labour and are burdened and I will refresh you'. One condition He always asks: Trust. No matter how weak you are, how frail. He will help if you will only go to Him. If anyone would really believe that God would make you a saint you would become one. We should have bigger hearts, more confidence. We don't trust Him one-tenth part as much as we should. Where do any good thoughts or aspirations we ever have come from? From Him; they are His gift. He says: 'If you will only let Me, I will make a saint of you'. It is by your want of confidence, hope, and trust, that you tie His hands.

Sympathy and the Want of it

There is hardly a greater power on earth than sympathy. The craving for sympathy is an ornament to our nature; God does not mean us to stand alone.

Our Lord Himself craved for sympathy, especially in His Agony, but also throughout His life on earth; yet how bitterly did He suffer for the want of it!

So may it often be with us. When we are suffering under any special unsatisfied craving of this kind, let us attach it to some particular want of sympathy endured by Our Lord in His Passion.

To have experienced the want of sympathy, and to have learnt to stand alone without it, should be of great value to us in our spiritual life:

1. If we do not get it on earth, we are forced to look from earth to heaven, for there we know is One who cannot change, and who knows perfectly all our sufferings and all our difficulties.

Indeed, there are certain natures with strong affections, of whom God seems to be jealous, desiring all that wealth of love for himself. From them he withdraws all earthly sympathy, so that they are compelled to turn to Him, who alone can satisfy them. Yet this turning to Him is not a thing to be done in one year – it is a long work, and it may take us several years before we learn to turn to Him wholly, to seek the sympathy we need from Him, to look on Him as our Consoler.

2. To be able to do without human sympathy, to face the want of such sympathy, makes us unselfish, for too great a craving for sympathy is but a form of selfishness.

3. By wanting sympathy and not getting it, we learn by

experience how to sympathise with others. No one is so well able to give sympathy as one who has known the want of it; one who wishes to save others from having to drink the cup which he has drunk.

Monotony

We must fight against our natural dislike of monotony by not casting our thoughts forward and thereby making the temptation stronger, foreseeing that tomorrow will be the same as today, and the next day the same as tomorrow, and so on.

Rather let us throw ourselves heartily into the work in hand, reminding ourselves that we know very little about the future, or even if we shall have a future, and making each day stand by itself as if it were the last one. God intends us to find life monotonous, for otherwise we should become too fond of it. It is one of His ways of bringing home to us our need of Him, and we should look on it and welcome it as a part of our education. The best cure for monotony in our own lives is to try and make life for others bright and cheerful.

Distractions in Prayer

It is not so much our mind as our heart that God wants in prayer. When the heart is not turned away from God, distractions (which are often purely physical) are not to be noticed or worried about.

That the mind should not be entirely fixed on God, even, for example, when reciting the Divine Office, is not incompatible at all with the spirit of prayer.

To resign myself to a distraction for God's sake is union with God.

The more we are united to God habitually, the more God reproves us, showing us the importance of little things, small faults against charity, slight negligence with regard to matters concerning which God has spoken to me about my soul, things God cares about in me, and if in these matters we do not behave well towards Him, we feel it in prayer and our communications with Him become difficult. As we improve and treat Him better, our communications become more easy. So, often, when I do not get the comfort in prayer that I hope for, it is but a sign of His true and special friendship, thus teaching me to see and guard against my own defects.

Injustice and the Value of a Grievance

Can any injustice I shall ever have to suffer come up to those which our Blessed Lord bore for my sake, and which He felt most acutely?

For love of Him let us keep our lips closed when we smart under the sense of injustice.

Two thoughts that will help us:

1. If we ourselves have ever been unjust to others, it

behoves us not to be too sensitive when others seem to be unjust to us.

2. If we were all of us to receive perfect justice, 'which of us would escape a whipping?' And should we then be so eager to put forward our claims?

To conquer ourselves in this matter, we must soothe and quiet our imagination. If we allow ourselves to brood on our grievances, the sense of injustice smouldering within us is apt to burst out. Don't let our minds dwell on these thoughts.

Speaking of a grievance always makes it worse, deepens it. Don't speak under vexation.

It may take us very high in the spiritual life to have a grievance and to say nothing about it but to God Himself. Such conduct will be the beginning of great progress: a quiet and unobtrusive way of going on to high virtue.

Antipathies

I should regard theose with whom I find it difficult to get on, as having been sent to help me to overcome myself; and towards them there is a special mission which I must fulfil. What a terrible thing if at our Judgment Our Blessed Lord were to say to us: 'You have been a difficulty in the way of N., who wanted to come to Me!' What could we answer?

Trials and Temptations

As long as there is nothing to fret one's temper there is not much interior movement towards perfection.

It is through trials, through tests, that we are enabled to practise virtues.

Temptation does not make us weak, but it tests us to show us if we are weak.

If the Devil sees someone striving seriously to overcome herself, he marks her out for attack.

In temptations to temper, it is well sometimes to put oneself into the occasion of exhibiting temper; and when the temptation is some antipathy, to try to be often with the person in question; for it is facing such trials, and overcoming them, that help to make us saints.

Our Blessed Lord was thwarted at every step, and if we want to model our lives on His, we shall welcome our trials, instead of complaining about them.

We must look on our spiritual life as one of great activity, full of energy, with a great deal going on in it from day to day. I must estimate the good days of my spiritual life by the struggles and tussles I have gone through. If I want to know how God judges of my earnestness, let me see how many times a week I have had an engagement with the enemy. A peaceful day has not added one stone to the spiritual edifice. I must strengthen my spiritual muscles by exercising them.

If, looking back, I can see that I have endured pain and overcome temptation, I know that I am advancing towards God. Do I take this view of life?

If I do I shall be inclined to envy those who have more trials to bear than I have myself.

God alone can give us light on this; accustom us to it till we regard a difficulty or a pain as a part of His training of us – a sign that He is taking us in hand and making something of us.

Not that we shall ever like trials, but we shall become better able to bear them, and the time may come when we shall receive them with joy.

Venial or Little Sins

Considering the sinfulness of little sins, remembering that whether a sin be mortal or venial, the Person against whom it is committed is the same.

And consider some of the effects of little sins:

1. They deprive us of the special providence and favour of God. By this special providence I mean that special care God takes of the soul in the midst of temptations; God keeping away difficulties; not allowing the Devil that power he would otherwise have; the felt companionship of God. What a priceless boon to be under this special providence, and what a pity to forfeit it!

In friendship a little matter may come between friends; so with God; if His friends do wilfully even some little thing against Him, He cannot help feeling it.

2. By little sins our spiritual senses become dulled. We do not see God in His creatures; in prayer we do not hear Him. If our hearing were good, God would only have to whisper and we should hear Him at once.

We have not realised till now, perhaps, the reason of our coldness and blindness – but if we are yielding to habitual venial sin, what wonder is it we cannot enjoy the union with God that we wish for!

3. By little sins we lose, or never acquire, that briskness and energy in doing God's work which were characteristics of the saints, even in sickness and old age. And where is our longing to make ourselves better? Habitual venial sin is the enemy of all these things. But when the soul is careful in avoiding venial sin, then it is that God's inspirations pour through every sense.

If you want to bear up against the lessons of life, avoid venial sin.

Sanctification

The first condition for carrying out God's Will in our regard – the sanctification of our soul – is to believe we can do it.

Three thoughts help us:

1. God is much more interested in our sanctification than we are ourselves. It is not man who goes to God

first, but God who comes to man, and as a beggar in this matter. It is not we who woo Our Blessed Lord, but He is the Lover who woos us. He takes it as a wonderful condescension on our part if we love Him. He cannot help loving us: 'Does a woman forget her baby at the breast, or fail to cherish the son of her womb? Yet even if these forget, I will never forget you. See, I have branded you on the palms of My hands.' (*Is* 49:15-16).

It is a part of God's perfection that He cannot help loving us, because we are His creatures. So God makes love to me, seeks me, and will not allow me to wander from Him.

2. We sometimes think past sins, near or far, must make it hopeless for us ever to attain to perfection. It is quite the contrary – we are forgiven in such a way that they no longer raise any obstacle between us and God. It is quite false to think that God bears us a grudge on account of the past. We should remember what poor weak wayward creatures we are, and just because we are so weak, it would not be fair of God to remember sins. 'He had compassion on the multitude.' That is God's feeling towards us, and when He sees us stumbling and tripping, He has the same pity for us as a mother has for her baby child.

3. God has a personal and special love for me, against which no argument can stand. God realises my weakness more than I do myself, pities me, and gives me any amount of time to correct my faults. Go back to the history of your life, make a chart of God's mercies, and

you will see at what pains He has been about you. Your
difficulties are leading you to perfection. Do a little each
day. Do well what is within your reach, and the rest will
come right. Perfection is gained by slow degrees. Have
no doubt that God will help you, and His goodness will
make all this possible for you.

Sorrow

A saint's sorrow is never in the way. There is about it a
softness, a sweetness, a gentleness, a beauty; it is a cross
only to himself. We must be careful, in sorrow, not to
demand sympathy from others, and if possible not to
crave for it. What is it worth if comes when we have
demanded it? There is no balm in it when it is paid to us
as a tax. Surely the preciousness lies in its being
spontaneous. This is not so much a question of what is
right or wrong, as of what is fittest and best, of what God
loves most, of what makes sorrow most heavenly. The
more consolation from creatures, the less from God. That
is the invariable rule. God is shy; He comes to the lonely
heart which other loves do not fill. This is why bereaved
hearts, outraged hearts, hearts misunderstood, hearts
which have broken with kith and kin and native place, are
the hearts of His predilection. Human sympathy is a dear
bargain. God waits outside till our company has gone.
Perhaps He cannot wait so long: He goes away, not
angrily but sadly ... and we, how much have we missed?

The Care of God for Me

Lose no opportunity in bringing home to yourself Our Lord's particular individual love of you, shown in even the smallest details of your life.

It is God's peculiar prerogative, because He alone is infinitely wise and all-powerful, to be able so to direct and rule each single life as if that person alone was the centre of the universe, and all things else were ordered for her advantage, solely and entirely.

When I rise in the morning I can say with truth: 'This day, in all its circumstances, with all its consequences, has been appointed and fashioned to help me to love and serve God better'. Then you have only to fall in with your changes of duties, or with the state of your health, or with the conduct of others towards you (which all has been foreseen and allowed for by God), secure in the knowledge that you are travelling along the path whereby God Himself wishes you to approach Him.

What peace, what courage, what an increase of love this thought should give us!

Sayings

When my heart gets into communication with God I have all that is needed.

The only distraction that counts is one of the heart.

God only wants my heart, and my desire to please Him.

To remain in God's presence, and to abandon myself to the pleasure of His presence, is excellent.

It is God's action in my soul that does me good, not the fine thoughts that come to my memory or imagination.

The Great Mystery

Man's craving always has been to see God, to think he is near Him, as far as possible to get into touch with Him; and therefore the aim of religion is to know God, to get upon intimate terms with Him, to see Him in all the ordinary actions of our lives, to live for Him, and to ask His help.

This recognition of God is the chief duty of man.

It constitutes our supreme happiness – this reaching forth beyond ourselves. This impulse to put forth our hand into the darkness to grasp the hand of our Divine Saviour, is common to all the human race, implanted in us by God himself.

God is always calling to us, always beckoning to us, and thus always giving us a proof of the infinite interest He takes in us, and of His love for us.

He is intended to be, He must always be, our Supreme Love. Of course He wishes us to find joy in this world, in the pure love of our fellow-creatures as well, if they do not shut out Him, and do not lead us into bondage to them. But even so, their power is only for a time; we wake as from a dream, and the old ache comes back, the old feeling of emptiness and dissatisfaction gnaws at our heart, and once more the cry breaks forth from our inmost being (very often a cry which we don't understand), 'It is not enough, I need more; only show me God, show me my Lord and my God'.

In merciful answer to this demand God, as we all know, came upon earth, and came in human form, spoke with a human voice, had a human appearance, because He was really a man. He moved up and down in Palestine, and wherever He went He was loved, except by those who for political and other reasons were His enemies. He was so humble, so simple, so accessible to everyone, that even His enemies said: 'The whole world has gone out after Him.' Yet they who had seen Him and heard Him could not and would not believe that the Lord of heaven and earth could have come down into our world, and have dwelt here, and have hung upon the Cross until He was dead, simply through love of them. But it was true. They disbelieved His love because it was so great.

But that same God is in the world still. He is in the world today although we have not the privilege which they had, who lived along with Him, of seeing Him with our bodily eyes and listening to His human voice.

He is God. He can do everything. Lay down before Him the burden of all your cares. Don't think He doesn't understand all about yourself. He alone does thoroughly understand you, because He made you, soul and body. He will either charm your sorrows away, or give you strength of mind and body to bear them. You will never find Him disappointing. He has all knowledge and all power, and He loves you more than you can believe.

You find life lonely. You find life with no relish in it. Go to Him, and He will make your life full of meaning, full of contentment, full of a steady joy.

And now you will ask: 'How am I to find in Him a friend? I want a friend badly, and one who won't change with the weather. A friend who will do me good. Someone to protect me in my hidden trials, who will always be patient with me, who will never tire of me when I am so tired of myself.'

Go to Him; but go to Him not only as to one who has a human heart, but who is also Very God of Very God.

Go to Him as to one who loves you, and if you only understand that a little better, it will explain everything and make everything easy.

He loves you too much to be able to be really angry with you. He only wants you to let Him heal your sores, and to give Him some excuse for forgiving you.

Don't think that He requires you to stand on ceremony with Him. You cannot be too simple, too childlike, to direct.

Why will you not believe His own speech? Why should He say He loves you if He does not do so in fact?

The shortest way to the mind and heart of God is to take Him at His word. A saint is a person who believes God's promises literally, and trusts them entirely and always. What is the explanation of this great mystery?

God who framed the heavens, caresses with baby hands the sweet face of His Mother – a woman – His own creature! He has made Himself a home upon earth!

Why was His infinite Power attracted by our weakness? Why was His Pity greater than our willfulness? Why has His Purity cleansed our sin? How was it that the Creator and the creature, Perfection and imperfection, Light and darkness, were thus brought together?

Not by constraint, because no one can constrain Almighty God. Not in His Wisdom, nor in His Greatness, nor in His Justice, will you find written the secret – why God created us, and dwelt and dwells amongst us.

One little word holds it all: the highest, dearest, best of all words; another word for God Himself – LOVE! GOD IS LOVE.

Approach Him by love; abide with Him in love. He wants you to live with Him now; to make a Friend of Him now. He wants you to let Him so take possession of your heart, that even while you are still living here your happiness may be in Him, your strength be founded on Him.

What has He left undone to prove His love for you?

What are you going to leave undone to prove your love for Him?